CW00407536

Brian Webb & Peyton Skipwith

Edward Bawden

DESIGN

Eric Ravilious

Antique Collectors' Club
in association with
The Fry Art Gallery
Saffron Walden

First published 2005
Reprinted 2008

ISBN 1 85149 500 2

British Library Cataloguing-in-Publication Data.
A catalogue record for this book is available from the British Library.

Antique Collectors' Club
www.antiquecollectorsclub.com

Sandy Lane, Old Martlesham,
Woodbridge, Suffolk IP12 4SD UK
Tel: 01394 389950 Fax: 01394 389999
Email:info@antique-acc.com
or
Eastworks, 116 Pleasant Street-Suite#18
Easthampton, MA 01027
USA Tel: (413) 529 0861 Fax: (413) 529 0862
Email:info@antiqueacc.com

Published by Antique Collectors' Club, Woodbridge, England
Design by Webb & Webb Design Limited, London
Printed and bound in China

Foreword

The Fry Art Gallery is managed by a Society of the same name, and since its creation in 1985 has been administered entirely by voluntary effort. So it was that Brian Webb in 2003 accepted an invitation to celebrate the centenary of the births of both Edward Bawden and Eric Ravilious by an exhibition of their work in design. This he did, with the assistance of Peyton Skipwith, and the support of the families of the artists. The Fry Art Gallery remains indebted to all concerned with that project for their support, which enabled its success. In the same year Brian Webb produced the first edition of this book, which was quickly sold out, and so we have proceeded to this enlarged and revised second edition. We are very grateful to Brian Webb and the design consultants Webb & Webb for professional help in this connection, and for support over the years.

Nigel Weaver
Chairman, The Fry Art Gallery

THE CHRISTMAS
BOOK SHOP

THE YEAR'S
BEST BOOKS

The Christmas Bookshop, an advertising insert for the December 1924 edition of the *Studio* was one of the earliest published designs drawn (and signed by both Ravilious and Bawden) whilst students at the Royal College of Art.

Design
Edward Bawden and Eric Ravilious

'The designs which Eric Ravilious made for industrial production are remarkable not only for their intrinsic excellence but also for the fact that to gain so much success he turned to his advantage two circumstances which might have been unpropitious; namely that as a wood engraver and as a painter he had established himself as an artist of first importance before ever he came to this work; and that he worked at a time when the invention of significant decorative designs was probably more difficult than at any preceding period in history.'
Thus, Richard Goodden began his memorial tribute in Architectural Review in December 1943.

Ravilious had been killed at the age of thirty-nine in an air-sea rescue mission fifteen months previously. Edward Bawden was to survive him by forty six years.

Both Ravilious' and Bawden's skills were honed in the Design School of the Royal College of Art, where, in the early 1920s, the craft ethic was strong; the tutors who taught there included Paul Nash, Edward Johnston and Harold Stabler. Ravilious' discipline was mural painting, whilst Bawden was assigned to book illustration. The pair became close friends, and it was whilst they were at the College that they began experimenting with print-making. Ravilious discovered the discipline of wood-engraving, whilst Bawden made his earliest essays in lino-printing. A cow that he cut one evening with a penknife evolved into *Tree and Cow*, one of his earliest wallpaper designs for the Curwen Press. The Curwen Press was to play a major role in the development of their design skills, and for Bawden particularly the steady demand for trade cards, head- and tail-pieces, swelled-rules, and border decorations provided the perfect vehicle for developing his extraordinary talent for pattern-making. Ravilious developed a fascination for lettering, which was at first exploited on the printed page, but was later to

become one of the defining symbols of the period. Nineteen-thirties style is epitomised by his alphabet china for Wedgwood and the Edward VIII Coronation Mug.

In addition to print-making and illustration, Bawden and Ravilious painted landscapes in watercolours and, in October 1927, shared an exhibition at the St George's Gallery with another close College friend, Douglas Percy Bliss. Their great break came, however, in 1928, when they were selected and commissioned, along with Charles Mahoney, to paint a mural for the Refreshment Room at Morley College in South London. The suggested subject-matter was 'London', which was quickly rejected in favour of 'fantasy'. This provided a challenge to their already fertile imaginations, but they achieved a popular success, which brought them considerable press-coverage and early recognition.

Concentration on the Morley College mural made them hunger for the countryside and a prolonged spell of landscape painting; this encouraged them to take their bicycles and explore rural Essex. In 1930 they came upon the village of Great Bardfield, where they were able to rent part of Brick House, which Bawden's father later bought for Edward and his wife Charlotte as a wedding present. This was the year Ravilious began work on the superb series of wood-engravings for the Golden Cockerel edition of Twelfth Night, and a visitor to Brick House recorded how he would sit 'by the window with his wood-cutting block of boxwood and a leather cushion under it - turning it this way and that as he went on cutting, and whistling all the time as beautifully as any bird - always on the in-breath, never the out.' (D P Bliss) Ravilious' exquisite cuts were much sought after by the publishers of fine editions, whilst Bawden's witty line-drawings were in demand as illustrations and dust-jackets for a wide range of popular works from the famous series of Shell advertisements to cookery books. No illustrator, before or since, could have persuaded an author or publisher, let alone the general public, that caterpillars and blue-bottles were suitable 'meat' for inclusion in such illustrations, but luckily for us Ambrose Heath and Faber had no such qualms.

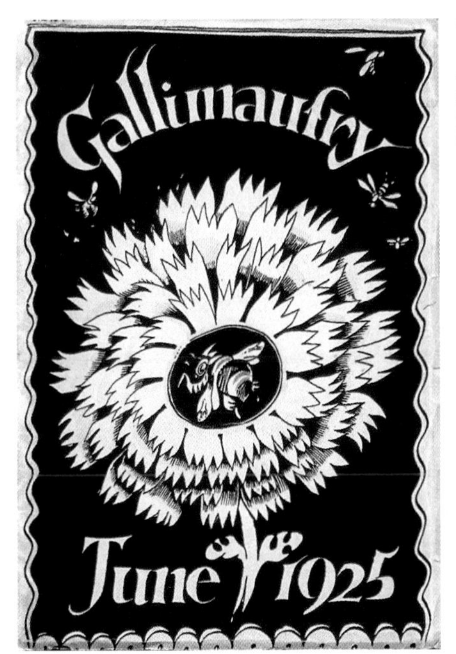

Two magazines published by the Common Room of the Royal College of Art. *Gallimaufry*, 1925, was edited by Douglas Percy Bliss. It contained engraved illustrations by Ravilious who also provided the cover, and hand coloured drawings by Bawden and wood engravings by Bliss and Enid Marx. The magazine states that *'the yellow'* on the cover *'was stencilled and the block will not be used again'*.

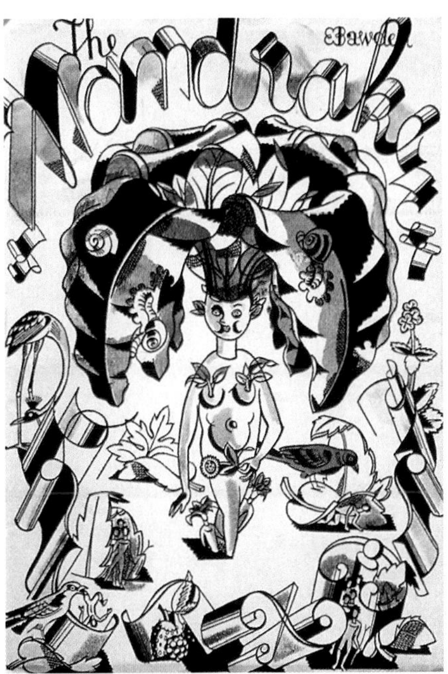

The Mandrake, in 1926, was edited by Cecilia Dunbar Kilburn (later Lady Sempill) and the cover illustrated by Bawden, with a title page engraving by Ravilious. The title page states an edition number of 200, *'coloured by hand and the whole put together in May MCMXXVI, the month of the great general strike'*.

Rather than just creating flat decoration to make existing wares, such as Wedgwood mugs, Ravilious, with his elegant, eighteenth-century style dining room furniture for Dunbar Hay was the first to experiment with three-dimensional design. But Bawden had experimented with industrial design, albeit on a cottage industry scale, from the time he left the College. His earliest tile-designs for Carter, Stabler and Adams (Poole Pottery) date from the 1920s, and in 1934 he produced an elegant design in black, blue and cream to decorate a biscuit tin of the young Princess Victoria visiting Tunbridge Wells. However, Bawden's great contribution to the style that, with hindsight, we now see as epitomising the ten or fifteen years immediately prior to the outbreak of World War II, is his wallpapers, ranging from the Curwen Papers - *Cow and Tree, Woodpigeon, Knole Park, Mermaid* and *Sahara*, through the Plaistow Papers, *Node* and *Facade*, to the Bardfield papers, done in conjunction with John Aldridge - *Periwinkle, Swan and Grasses, Stone Ivy* and *Grid and Cross*. Ravilious' contribution was the china. The *Boat Race* bowl, the alphabet mugs, the tea and dinner services, *Tea Time, Persephone* and *Garden*, with those lovely vignettes of tools, frames, swimming pools and green-houses, are perennial joys, whilst the Edward VIII coronation mug - quickly adapted for King George VI - with its exuberant lettering and effusion of fireworks is a design classic. Bawden, too, was to work with Wedgwood, but after the war, creating tableware for shipping lines - P&O and the New Zealand Shipping Company - but unlike Ravilious his experiences of working with the company were not happy.

In many ways The Festival of Britain marked the zenith of Ravilious/Bawden style. Although Ravilious had been dead for nine years, design and production had been in suspense for the duration, so this national celebration was like the coming of Spring after the long cold Winter of war and hardship. Bawden decorated the Lion and Unicorn Pavilion, whilst the following year saw the production of his *Heartsease* china for P&O, and a related curtain fabric, similarly printed in mauve and grey, for use on the RMS Oronsay. At roughly the same time Heals produced a fabric to his design created specifically for the Time-Life Building in New Bond Street, which was opened with great fanfares during coronation week in June 1953. Ravilious had also produced a few designs for textiles at the very end of his life but, ironically, the best known consists of a posthumous adaptation by Edinburgh Weavers of motifs taken from his Wedgwood lemonade set. The coronation provided a further excuse for Wedgwood to re-issue yet again his coronation mug; little alteration was required to adapt the original EVIIIR monogram to that of the new Queen.

Because Bawden lived over twice as long as his friend, he had more opportunities to exploit and utilise his design skills. Murals, cast-iron garden furniture for the Bilston Iron Foundry, beer bottle labels for Peter Walker's Warrington Ales, ingenious advertising material for Fortnums, mats and a tray for Gilbey's Gin, a cake box for Irish Air Lines - alas, not used - posters for London Transport, Imperial Airways and Ealing Studios and, in the late 1970s, the Bunyan Tapestry for the Cecil Higgins Art Gallery, Bedford. He revelled in the variety and challenge of these commissions.

Neither Bawden nor Ravilious compartmentalized their work. The practice of painting and printmaking proved far from unpropitious for both of them; they exploited the discipline of these crafts, which they allowed to inform their approach to other commissions, and vice-versa. As designers they were able to stand outside the art-politics, which embroiled many of their contemporaries: the clash of the Modernists versus Traditionalists; the battles of abstraction against naturalism, were of no particular concern to them. They invented patterns to suit the given brief, whether realistic, fantastic or pure; these were just vital variations of the artist-designer's rich visual language, the basic vocabulary of which they had learnt as students in the Design School at the Royal College of Art.

Peyton Skipwith

Described as a 'novel cover' for publisher William Heinemann's 1925 *Autumn List* and used as a supplement to *Commercial Art* in November 1925. Edward Bawden's name also appears, together with that of Ravilious, in an advertisement for the Artists' Agent RP Gossop in the same issue of the magazine. Bawden arrived at the Royal College of Art in 1922 with a Royal Exhibition for writing and illuminating but said he learnt to use a fine brush instead of a pen doing "tiddley jobs for Curwen".

A unique lino-cut and mono print produced by Bawden while still a student at the Royal College of art and given to a friend c.1924.

Similar fish not only appear in designs for Poole Potteries, but also later in *Wave* wallpaper, 1929. Lithographed at Curwen Press from lino-cuts.

Pottery Making at Poole, 1925. Harold Stabler, a director of Poole Potteries, became an early patron. Bawden designed booklets and maps for the firm which in turn led to a long term association with Harold Curwen at the Curwen Press. In 1932 Poole produced a series of painted tiles based on illustrations from *Pottery Making at Poole* to decorate their company canteen.

Woodpigeon (also known as *Church and Dove*). Wallpaper from a number of designs including *Seaweed*, *Sahara*, *Mermaid* and *Tree and Cow*. Lithographed at Curwen Press from lino-cuts, 1925-27, and sold by the sheet at Modern Textiles and The Little Gallery.
Edward Bawden used his wallpapers, including *Woodpigeon,* to decorate his house in Park Lane, Saffron Walden.

Art Galleries and *Association Football.* Press advertisements for the Underground 1928. Bawden's early illustrations show his interest in the drawings of Edward Lear and the Nash brothers, Paul and John.

Watercolour design for the Refreshment Room murals at Morley College, c.1928, illustrating *The Tempest*, with the English Channel as a background. Bawden placed the drawing with other work down his well in Brick House garden for safety before going off in 1940 to serve as a war artist.

April Fools. Jacket illustration for Compton Mackenzie's 1930 novel. published by Cassell. The foreground figure is possibly a self-portrait.

The Bibliolaters Relaxed. Menu printed and stencilled in colour at Curwen Press for the Double Crown Club dinner sixteen, 1928. Inside Bawden reinterprets the imprints of well known publishers, the Golden Cockerel, Chatto & Windus, the Nonesuch Press and Pelican Press.

Before and after. 1935 menu for the Double Crown Club dinner forty-eight. *After* shows James Laver, the speaker, trying to make himself heard, with Barnett Freedman and possibly Ravilious in the foreground and Bawden drawing the scene on the left.

Head-piece illustrations for the 1935 *Kynoch Press Note Book.*

Head-pieces for Westminister Bank advertisements, c.1935.

Kew Gardens, 1936 poster for London Underground. One of the many posters designed by Bawden for London Transport over a 30 year period. Printed lithographically at Curwen Press from lino-cuts.

May Brick House garden, 1932. Line drawings from *Good Food*, the first of Ambrose Heath's cookery books for Faber & Faber. Eric Ravilious and Thomas Hennell are on the left and Edward Bawden and Tirzah Ravilious on the right.

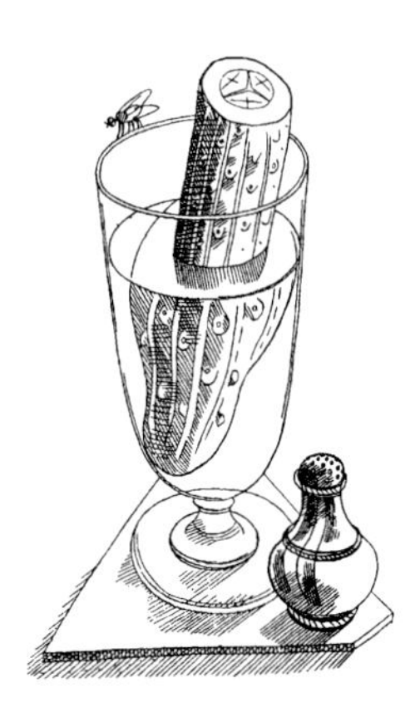

Routledge, 1925

Faber & Gwyer, 1928

Faber & Faber, 1931

Faber & Faber, 1933

Edward Bawden designed and illustrated more than one hundred

Faber & Faber, 1935

John Lehmann n.d.1940s

Hamish Hamilton, 1945

Chatto & Windus, 1956

book jackects and publications over a fifty year period.

Good Drinks, title page, 1939.

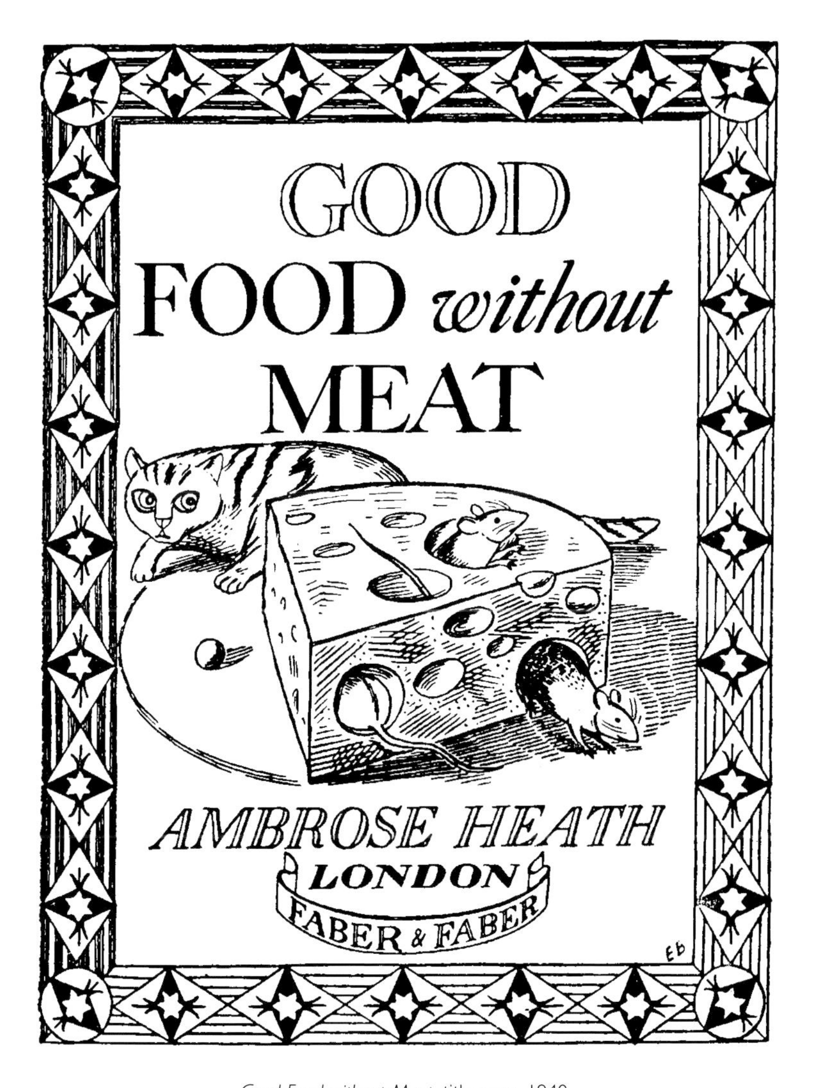

Good Food without Meat, title page, 1940.

The Zoo line drawing from the *Week-end Book* published by the Nonesuch Press, 1939, demonstrates all of Bawden's skills as a draughtsman, decorative artist and lettering designer.

English Garden Delights mural designed for the *RMS Orcades*, 1947. Painted as a series of nine panels each measuring 83 ins x 28 ins (210 cm x 72cm).

LLANFAIRPWLLGWYNGYLLGOGERYCHWYRNDROBWLL-LLANTYSILIOGOGOGOCH

BUT **SHELL** ***LLASTS LLONGEST***

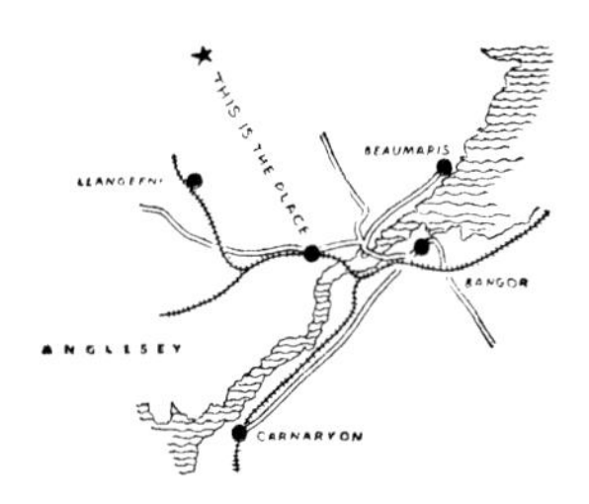

YOU CAN BE SURE OF SHELL

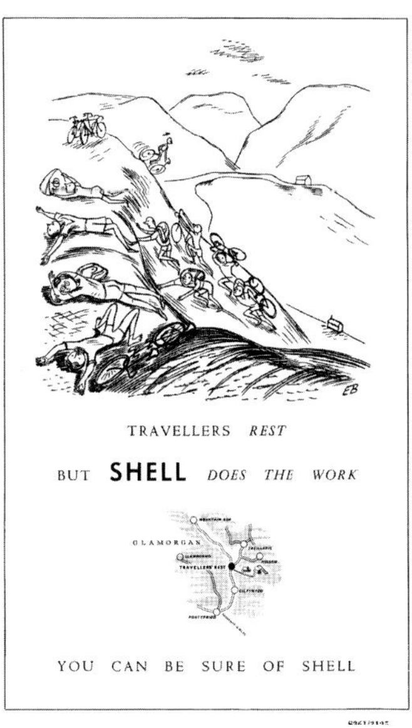

Bawden's drawings began a long series of *'You can be sure of Shell'* advertisements in the early 1930's. John Betjeman who worked for a time at ShellMex wrote some, if not all of the copy lines.

Front and back covers for the company's history, celebrating 125 years of Barrows, Birmingham, Lithograph, 1949.

Ascot, line drawing for Vogue, c.1948.

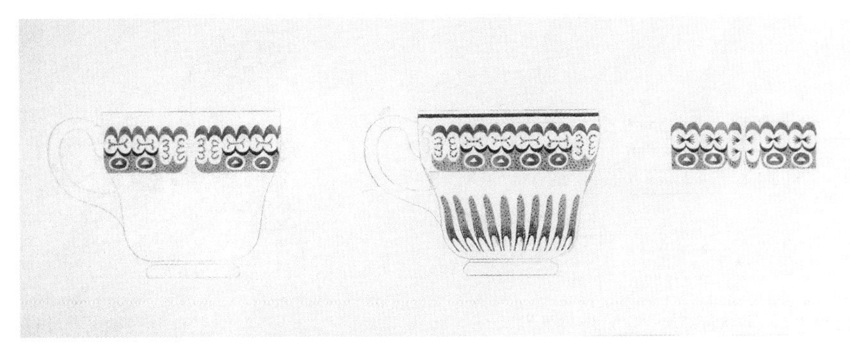

Heartsease ceramic designs for the Orient Shipping Line, 1952, manufactured by Wedgwood. Pencil, ink and watercolour. Bawden recorded his working relationship with Wedgwood as less happy than that of Ravilious.

Lino-cut and hand lettered designs for Peter Walker's Warrington *Pale Ale* bottle labels, 1952. These and designs for Brown Peter Ale and Walker's Stout were commissioned and the finished labels printed by Curwen Press.

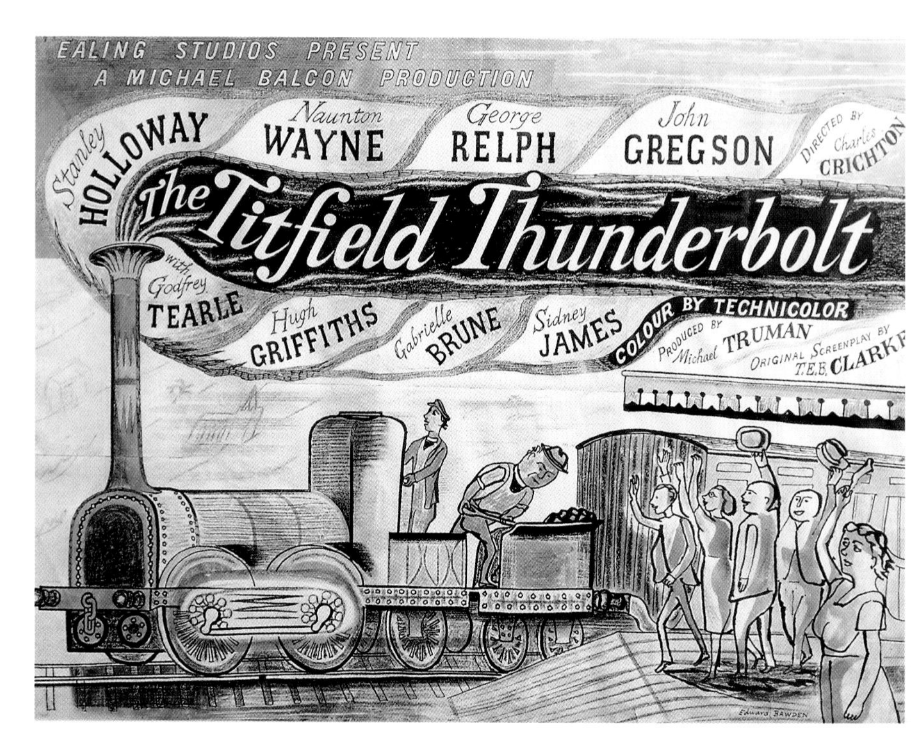

The engine used in Ealing Studio's *Titfield Thunderbolt* film was The Lion, made in Leeds in 1838. Bawden's poster, based on the engine, was produced in landscape and portrait formats, the artwork drawn in coloured crayons with added watercolour. The film, directed by Charles Crichton and written by TEB Clarke, tells the story of a village fighting the closure of its branch line. The poster and Christmas card below, were produced in 1953.

Watercolour designs for the proposed decimal currency introduced in 1971. Bawden's proposals, c.1962, illustrating national and traditional peace symbols were rejected.

Cut-to-shape *Easter Catalogues* for Fortnum & Mason, c.1955.

Fortnum & Mason *Christmas Catalogues*, 1955, 1956 and 1958, commissioned by the advertising agents Colman Prentice and Varley. Father Christmas is illustrated as Bawden's favourite animal in the 1958 version which becomes a CATalogue with a title page poem ending *The Christmas Cat perused each page and found new friends at every stage.*

Fortnum's a-flutter for Easter, 1958 Easter catalogue in a die-cut 'hen coop' sleeve. The chickens hatch as the catalogue is removed from the sleeve.

Above and below, artwork for decorations to Fortnum's *Friends Overseas*, Christmas 1955.

Design for a garden urn, pencil. Ink and watercolour. c.1955.

Collaged lino-cut design for a tile panel, Highbury and Islington Underground Station c.1955. London Transport Victoria Line.

Frontispiece engraving for Martin Armstrong's *Desert, a Legend,* 1926, published by Jonathan Cape. After this, his first illustrated book, Ravilious quickly learned to open up his engravings for trade publications.

Tail-piece engravings for a limited edition version of Nicholas Breton's *The Twelve Moneths,* reprinted from Breton's *Fantasticks*, 1626 and published by Robert Gibbing's Golden Cockerel Press, 1927.

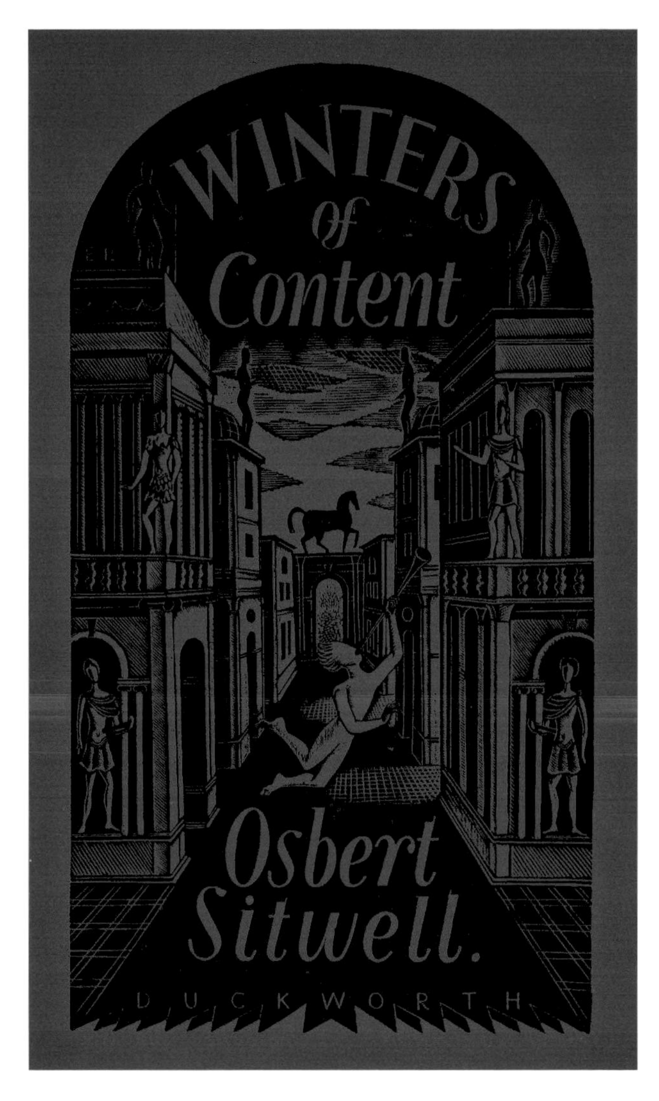

Engraved jacket design for *Winters of Content*, by Osbert Sitwell, 1932, published by Duckworth, printed on red uncoated paper.

Twelth Night one of Ravilious' most celebrated limited editions for Golden Cockerel, 1932 in which the engravings were printed in colour, much to his disapproval.

Monotype Calendar 1933. Wood engravings printed in two colours, for a typographical calendar commissioned by Beatrice Warde for the Monotype Corporation.

DECEMBER 1933

SUNDAY	Nov. 26	3	10	17	24	31	SUNDAY
MONDAY	Nov. 27	4	11	18	25	Jan. 1	MONDAY
TUESDAY	Nov. 28	5	12	19	26	Jan. 2	TUESDAY
WEDNESDAY	Nov. 29	6	13	20	27	Jan. 3	WEDNESDAY
THURSDAY	Nov. 30	7	14	21	28	Jan. 4	THURSDAY
FRIDAY	1	8	15	22	29	Jan. 5	FRIDAY
SATURDAY	2	9	16	23	30	Jan. 6	SATURDAY

THE MONOTYPE CORPN LTD, 43 FETTER LANE, E.C.4 :: POLIPHILUS 170

ILLUSTRATIONS ARE FROM ORIGINAL WOOD-ENGRAVINGS BY ERIC RAVILIOUS

Monotype Calendar 1933. Each 220mm x 140mm card is set in a different typeface as an example of Monotype's range.

Preliminary drawing in pencil and watercolour and final wood engraving for the Golden Cockerel Press prospectus 1931.

One of four engravings from *The Famous Tragedy of the Jew of Malta*, published by the Golden Hours Press, 1933.

Head-piece engravings for the 1933 Kynoch Press Note Book.

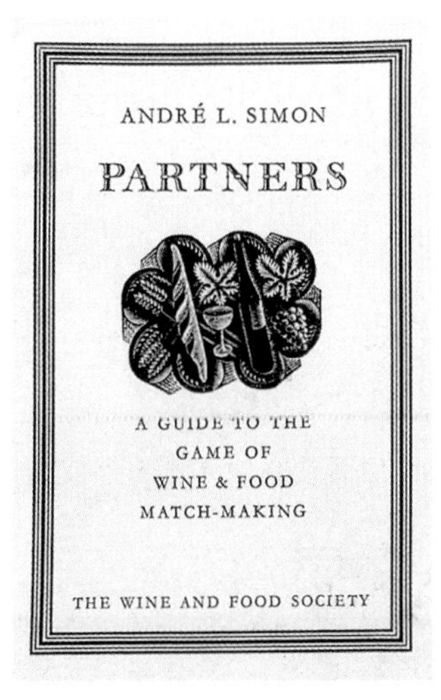

by

ERIC RAVILIOUS

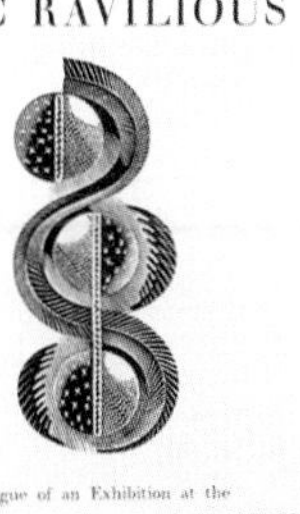

Catalogue of an Exhibition at the

ZWEMMER GALLERY

26 Litchfield Street, W.C.2

NOVEMBER 24th–DECEMBER 16th, 1933

WITH EASTER COMPLIMENTS
FROM THE CORNHILL
1934

Booklet and catalogue covers using commissioned and 'stock' engravings, 1930's.

Double Crown Club menu, 1935, based on the actual menu, the lettering is engraved over a dover sole.

Catherine Wheel, c.1935, Curwen Press 'stock' block. Fireworks recur throughout Ravilious's work in paintings and engravings.

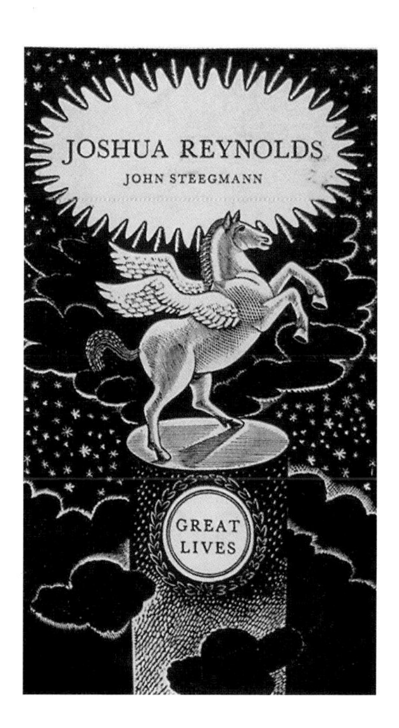

Pegasus on a pedestal. Wood engravings for Duckworth's *Great Lives* series, number 1, Shakespeare and number 5, Joshua Reynolds. Printed black on a variety of tinted papers. First published 1933.

Cecilia Dunbar, a contemporary of Ravilious and Bawden at the Royal College of Art founded *Dunbar Hay* with Athole Hay in 1935. The 'doll's house' wood engraved trade card illustrates giant scale furniture, glass, ceramics, cutlery and a ribbon of wallpaper.

Described as a design for a carpet by Cecilia Dunbar and commissioned c.1935 for Dunbar Hay. This design seems not to have been put into production. The central motif of figs is surrounded by decorations of strawberries, cherries, hops (twice) and a note indicating *cassis*. Watercolour with ribbon border and sponged fringe.

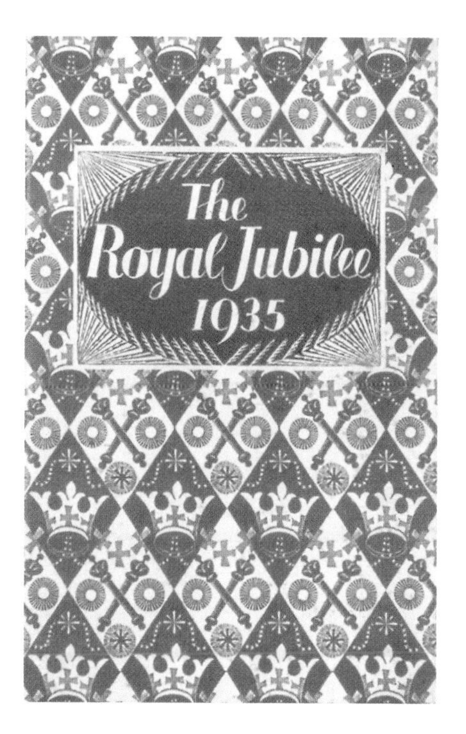

Thrice Welcome, A booklet to celebrate the Royal Jubilee, 1935 containing three essays: the Beauty of Southern England by S P B Mais, The Social and Sporting Season by Charles Graves and The Birthplace of English History by D I Frazer Harris. Wood engraving, cover printed in two colours and title page vignette in black for Southern Railways. Printed by Curwen Press.

Garden, 1939. Pencil and watercolour design for Wedgwood. Earlier Ravilious had complained that Wedgwoods thought "my beautiful designs above the heads of their public". He went on to say "Old Josiah's (Wedgwood) patterns are the most perfect pottery designs I've seen and they molder here because they haven't wide appeal either".

Oval serving plate. *Garden* was made in a variety of dinner, tea and coffee services and in several colourways.

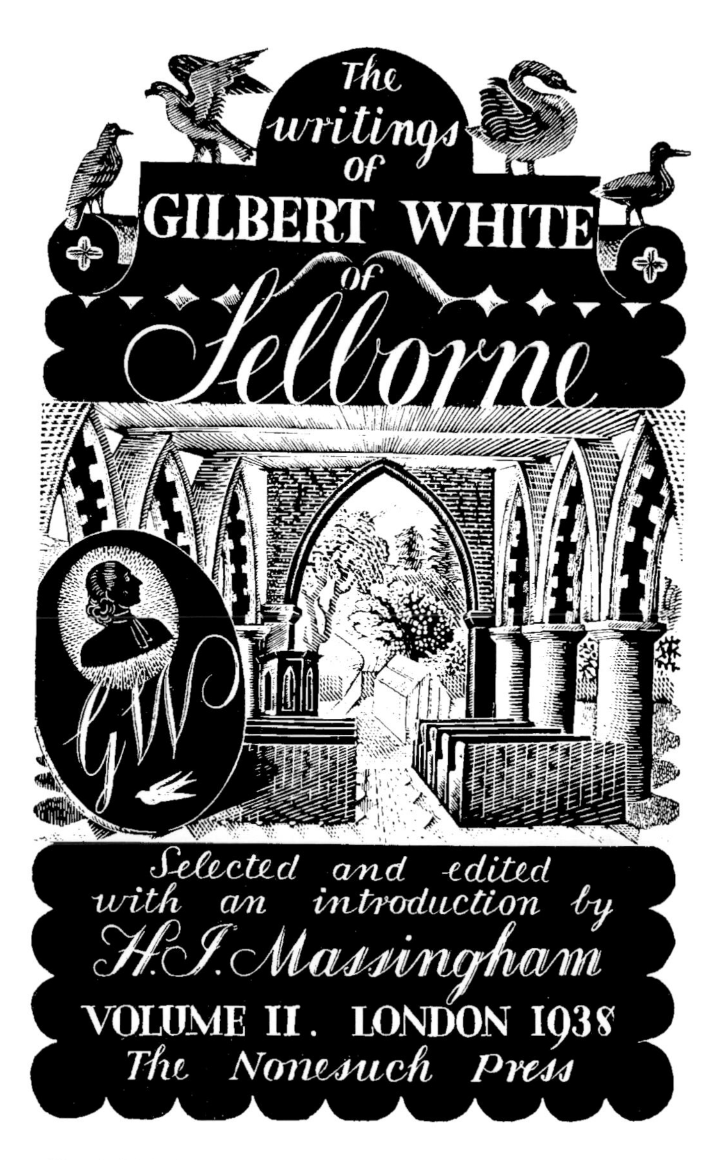

Gilbert White's *Selborne* was the last major engraved work by Ravilious, the book was published in two volumes in 1938 by the Nonesuch Press.

Title page engraving for what is now Ravilious' best known book, *High Street*, a 'trade' book of lithographed shops with a commentary by the archtectural writer J M Richards, published in 1938 by Country Life.

Engraving for London Transport, Green Line buses, illustrating some of Ravilious' favourite images, greenhouses and tea tables, 1935.

Beautiful Britain a three colour lithograph with drawn lettering for the cover of the 1939 Country Life Calendar. Printed by Morrison and Gibb.

Catalogue covers for the British Pavilion at the New York World Fair. The 1939 blocks were cut before the outbreak of the Second World War and the publication was heavily revised and a new 1940 block cut.
Ravilious had resisted "another coat of arms" and produced a design based on Britannia. In a letter to AJA Symons he explains that it was rejected in favour of the coat of arms.

Wisden Cricketer's Almanack, engraved in 1938 (and still in use).

Watercolour design for one of a small number of textiles commissioned by the Cotton Board in 1941 as a way of persuading cotton manufacturers to produce economical fabrics in wartime conditions. Ravilious' notes list alternative letters and colourways.

English Wits. Jacket and title page engraving. A compendium of brief biographies of writers including (Irish) Oscar Wilde and Max Beerbohm, for Hutchinson, 1940.

Noel, 1939, lithographed and hand painted Christmas plate for Wedgwood. Wartime conditions brought the projected production of the set to a halt.

Watercolour and pencil design for a garden pergola 1930s. The finial, Ravilious notes, is a pair of walking sticks.

Some of Ravilious' favourite national symbols and architectural illuminations combine to illustrate the lithographed bookjacket of *London Fabric* published by Batsford in 1939.

Coronation mugs, 1936, 1937 and 1953. The King Edward VIII mug was Ravilious' first commission for Wedgwood. It was revised for King George VI and again after Ravilious' death, for Queen Elizabeth II.

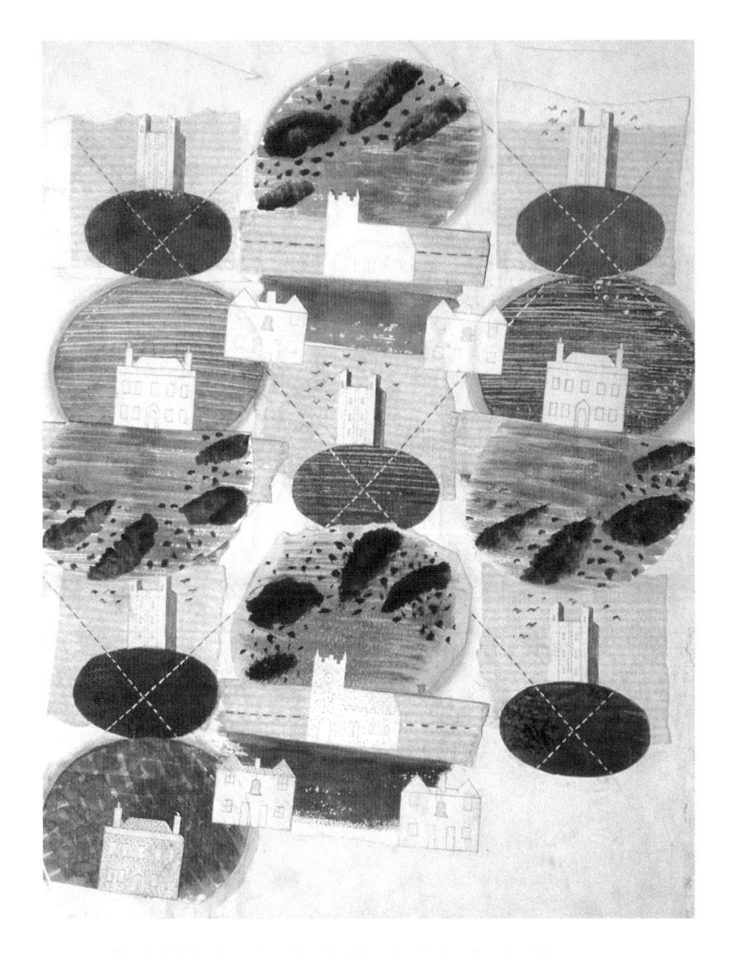

Castle Hedingham Landmarks. Textile design for the Cotton Board, 1941. Having originally shared Brick House with Edward and Charlotte Bawden in Great Bardfield, Ravilious moved with his wife Tirzah and children to Castle Hedingham in 1934.

Alphabet, Nursery ware for Wedgwood, 1937. The range includes cereal bowls, plates, milk jugs, lamp base and double ended egg cup for duck and hen eggs.

Childrens' handkerchief, the only Ravilious design for the Cotton Board to be produced. Lithographic proof on paper c.1941.

Descriptive devices for Dent's *Everyman* series in use between 1935 and 1953.

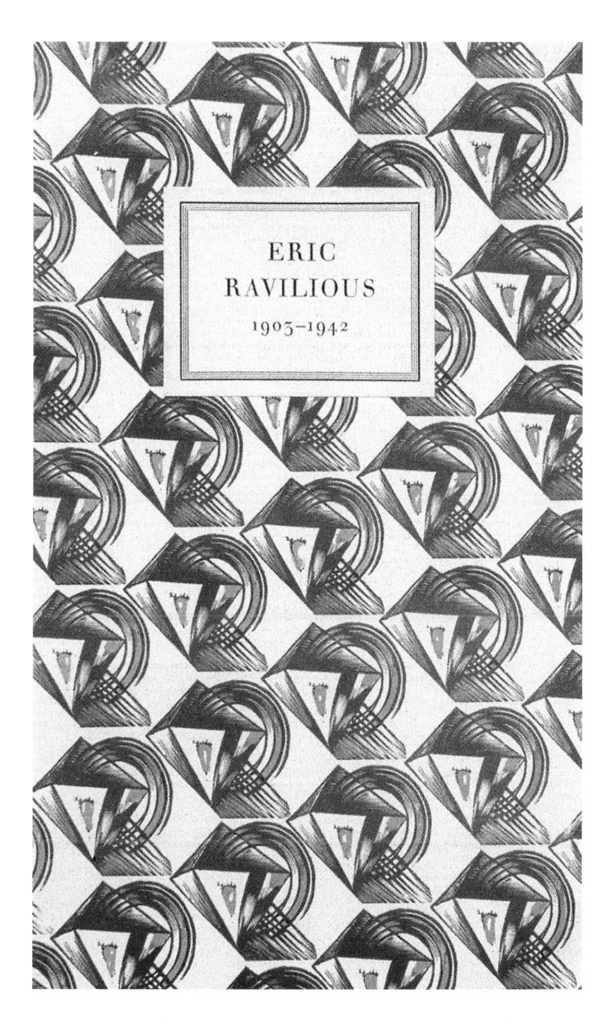

Eric Ravilious 1903-1942. Catalogue for the memorial exhibition organised by the Arts Council 1948-9. Printed by Curwen Press, the cover used the block cut for his first illustrated book *Desert* and later re-used as a Curwen pattern paper. The face used for the title is Walbaum, Curwen's 'trademark' type.

Chronology in order of seniority

Edward Bawden

Born in Braintree, Essex. 10 March 1903

1909 Cambridge School of Art

1922 Design School, Royal College of Art, meets Eric Ravilious
Meets Harold Curwen, Curwen Press

1924 Poster designs for London Transport and British Empire Exhibition

1925-26 Travelling scholarship to Italy. Designs for Poole Potteries and Curwen Press, Twinings Teas, Westminster Bank, London Transport. RCA Magazines *Gallimaufry* and *The Mandrake* published (with Ravilious)

1927-29 Copper engravings, wallpaper designs

1928 Work starts on Morley College murals. Teaching at Goldsmiths and RCA. Illustrations for *The Life and Adventures of Peter Wilkins*

1930 Illustrations for *Adam and Evelyn at Kew*. Designs for Faber & Faber, Barrows, Birmingham, LNER. Morley College murals unveiled by Stanley Baldwin

1932 Marries Charlotte Epton. Shell advertising. Illustrations for *Good Food*

1933 First one-man exhibition at Zwemmer Gallery. Illustrations for *More Good Food*

1934 Designs for Pavilion Hotel, Scarborough

1935 Illustrations for *Good Soups*, *Good Potato Dishes* and *Kynoch Press Note Book*

1936 London Transport, *Kew Gardens*, *Hyde Park* and *St James' Park* Posters

1939 Illustrations for *The Weekend Book*.
Bardfield wallpapers with John Aldridge

1940-45 Appointed Official War Artist with the rank of Honorary Captain. Evacuated from Dunkirk. Travels in Middle East

1946 CBE, Associate of Royal Academy

1947 Illustrations for *The Arabs*

1948 Illustrations for *Gulliver's Travels* and *Vogue*
Designs for Coles and Sons wallpapers.
Hue and Cry, Ealing Studios posters

1949 Teaching in Canada. Awarded Royal Designer for Industry by The Royal Society of Arts. Illustrations for *Life in an English Village* and *London is London*

1950-51 *Lion and Unicorn* mural at the Festival of Britain

1952 Murals for the RMS *Orcades* and RMS *Oransay*. Heartsease designs for Orient Line manufactured by Wedgwood.
Beer bottle labels for Peter Walker

1953 Illustrations for *The Queens Beasts*. Designs for Royal Hotel Scarborough and Selfridges in celebration of the Coronation. *Titfield Thunderbolt* Ealing Studios posters

1955 Designs for Fortnum & Mason

1957 Elected RA. Designs for *Bilston* garden furniture

1958 Murals for Morgan Crucible and Brussels Exhibition. Second mural for Morley College. Designs for Edinburgh Tapestry Co.

1960-61 Mural for *Empress of Canada*

1962-63 Murals for Hull University, children's book *Hold fast by your teeth* published. Designs for decimal currency (rejected)

1964 Society of Industrial Artists Silver Medal

1965 Murals for Pilkington Brothers and Queen's University, Belfast

1966 Murals for British Petroleum and British Pavilion, Expo66, Montreal

1967 Illustrations for OUP *Old Testament*.
Six *London Markets* prints

1968-72 Tile panels for London Transport, Victoria Line

1972-73 *Edward Bawden's Oxford* for Blackwells

1977 Gold medal for *Utopia*, Leipzig. Silver medal for *Rasselas* V&A Museum

1978 75th Birthday Exhibition at the Fine Art Society London

1979 *Lady Filmy Fern* published (started 1935 completed 1979)

1987 Illustrations for *The Hound of the Baskervilles*

1988 Retrospective exhibition at V&A Museum

1989 Dies 21 November lino-cutting in Saffron Walden

Edward Bawden drew innumerable illustrations for more than seventy books and over one hundred book jackets and publications.
The chronology lists dates of publication.

Eric Ravilious

Born in Acton, London, 22 July 1903

1919 Eastbourne School of Art

1922 Design School, Royal College of Art. Meets Edward Bawden. Tutors include Paul Nash

1924 Awarded Design School scholarship to Italy

1925 Final year at RCA. Proposed for Society of Wood Engravers by Paul Nash

1926 Teaching at Eastbourne School of Art, meets Tirzah Garwood. Wood engravings for *Desert*

1927 Engravings for a *A Ballad upon a Wedding* and *The Twelve Moneths*

1928 Designs for Morley College murals. Teaching at RCA

1929 Engravings for *Monotype Almanack* and *Atrocities of Pirates*. Work published in *The Woodcut*. 5th July marries Tirzah

1930 Morley College murals unveiled. Portrait of Bawden (now in the Senior Common Room, RCA)

1932 Engravings for *Twelfth Night*, *Consequences* and *Winters of Content*
Shares Brick House, Great Bardfield with the Bawdens

1933 Engravings for *The Famous Tragedy of the Rich Jew of Malta*, *54 Conceits*, *Monotype Calendar* and *Kynoch Press Note Book*

1934 Moves to Castle Hedingham. Mural for Pier Pavilion, Colwyn Bay

1935 Engravings for *The Hansom Cab and the Pigeons*, *Thrice Welcome*, *Everyman Library*, *Double Crown Club Menu*, advertisements for Green Line Buses, trial designs for Wedgwood. Textiles and furniture designs for Dunbar Hay

1936 Engravings for *Poems by Thomas Hennell*, Trade card for Dunbar Hay, *Country Walks* for London Transport. Designs for Edward VIII Coronation mug. Second one-man show at Zwemmers

1937 Engravings for *Country Life Cookery Book*. Catalogue and tennis exhibit for Paris International Exhibition. Work starts on *High Street* lithographs

1938 Engravings for *Natural History of Selborne* and *Wisden Cricketer's Almanack*

1939 Exhibition at Tooths, designs for postage stamps (rejected)

1940 Appointed Official War Artist with the rank Honorary Captain, Royal Marines. Painting in Sheerness, Grimsby, Norway. Exhibition of War Artists work at National Gallery

1941 Submarine lithographs exhibited at Leicester Galleries. Textiles for Cotton Board. Painting in Dover and Scotland

1942 Painting in Essex, Hertfordshire and Somerset. 22nd August flies to Iceland

2nd September fails to return from rescue mission, reported missing, presumed dead

Eric Ravilious engraved more than four hundred illustrations and drew over forty lithographic designs for books and publications. The chronology lists dates of publication.

The Fry Art Gallery was opened in 1987 to display work by artists of repute who had close associations, during the 20th century, with North West Essex, where Saffron Walden is situated. Within a small compass there was an exceptional gathering of talent, that might have equalled St Ives had they formally allowed themselves to be seen as a school. Instead the artists who gathered in the village of Great Bardfield, near Saffron Walden, between 1930 and 1970 were steadfast in their refusal to be seen in this way, although the influence of Edward Bawden in attracting talented Royal College of Art graduates to move there (like Bernard Cheese, Sheila Robinson, Walter Hoyle), and the constant presence of John Aldridge RA, meant that a similarity of interest in the English landscape united them. They also often had a common interest in printmaking and in watercolour. Eric Ravilious, who had lived in the village until shortly after his marriage to Tirzah Garwood, then moved to nearby Castle Hedingham, had died in 1942, but his friend Kenenth Rowntree remained for some years, and they were joined by Michael Rothenstein RA and his wife (the painter Duffy Ayers) as well as Marianne Straub, textile designer, Audrey Cruddas, stage designer, George Chapman, and Stanley Clifford-Smith. John Norris Wood, Richard Bawden and Chloe Cheese grew up there.

During the 1950s four open studio days were held, creating a great deal of national interest. Nearby, at various times during these years, but never part of the loose confederation that became the Great Bardfield Artists' Association, lived Michael Ayrton, Isabel Lambert, Robert Colquhoun and Robert MacBryde, whilst Edwin Smith and Olive Cook were frequent visitors until they settled permanently in Saffron Walden. Bawden ultimately spent the last eighteen years of his life in the town, and was an early supporter of the gallery, as well as a generous benefactor. All these artists, and others who lived in Saffron Walden, form the North West Essex Collection, the raison d'être of The Fry Art Gallery.

Nigel Weaver
Chairman

The Fry Art Gallery
www.fryartgallery.org

Bridge-End Gardens, Castle Street,
Saffron Walden, Essex CB10 1BD
Telephone 01799 513779